LET'S LOOK AT COUNTRIES

LET'S LOOK AT

AUSTRALIA

BY A. M. REYNOLDS

raintree
a Capstone company — publishers for children

Raintree is an imprint of Capstone Global Library Limited, a company incorporated in England and Wales having its registered office at 264 Banbury Road, Oxford, OX2 7DY – Registered company number: 6695582

www.raintree.co.uk
myorders@raintree.co.uk

Edited by Erika L. Shores
Designed by Juliette Peters
Original illustrations © Capstone Global Library Limited 2020
Picture research by Jo Miller
Production by Kathy McColley
Originated by Capstone Global Library Ltd
Printed and bound in India

ISBN 978 1 4747 6946 4 (hardback)
ISBN 978 1 4747 6964 8 (paperback)

British Library Cataloguing in Publication Data
A full catalogue record for this book is available from the British Library.

Acknowledgements
We would like to thank the following for permission to reproduce photographs: iStockphoto: AnnaGreen, 17, davidf, 11; Shutterstock: AustralianCamera, 6, Chris Howey, Cover Middle, Darren Tierney, 1, edella, 3, Edward Haylan, 7, Globe Turner, 22 (Inset), Greg Brave, Cover Bottom, Cover Back, Happy Auer, 12, kwest, 22-23, 24, Lucie Lang, 9, Marcel van den Bos, 15, Maurizio De Mattei, 21, nate, 4, NaturalBox, 13, Neale Cousland, 14, 19, Photodigitaal.nl, 8, SF photo, 5, Thomas Edmondson, Cover Top

Every effort has been made to contact copyright holders of material reproduced in this book. Any omissions will be rectified in subsequent printings if notice is given to the publisher.

All the internet addresses (URLs) given in this book were valid at the time of going to press. However, due to the dynamic nature of the internet, some addresses may have changed, or sites may have changed or ceased to exist since publication. While the author and publisher regret any inconvenience this may cause readers, no responsibility for any such changes can be accepted by either the author or the publisher.

CONTENTS

Where is Australia? 4

From deserts to rainforests 6

In the wild 8

People 10

At the table 12

Melbourne Cup 14

At work 16

Transport 18

Famous place 20

Quick Australia facts 22

Glossary 22

Find out more 23

Comprehension questions 24

Index 24

Where is Australia?

Australia is both a country and a continent. It is nearly 33 times bigger than the UK. Australia's capital is Canberra.

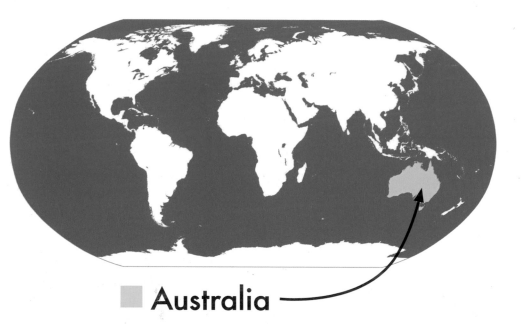

■ Australia

Canberra, Australia

From deserts to rainforests

Most of Australia is desert called the outback. Much of the country has no rain for many months. Rainforests grow in wet areas near the coasts.

In the wild

Australia is full of wildlife. Koalas climb trees. Kangaroos hop through the grass. Sharks swim in the seas. Deadly snakes and spiders live throughout Australia.

Australian king brown snake

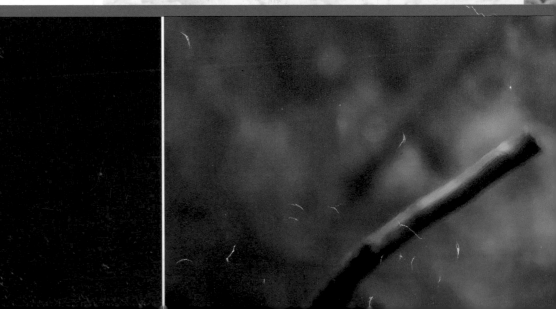

koala

People

Aboriginal people have lived in

Australia for 50,000 years.

In the 1700s, people came

from England and other countries

in Europe to live in Australia.

At the table

Australians eat a lot of meat. Many people like to eat outdoors. They cook meat on barbecues. They also like to eat meat pies!

Melbourne Cup

Australia holds a horse race called the Melbourne Cup every year. People from many countries enter horses in the race. People watch big screens to see which horse wins.

Fans watch the Melbourne Cup on a large outdoor screen.

At work

Many Australians work in offices, hospitals and shops.

Some people work in mines.

Workers called drovers look after sheep and cattle on large farms.

Transport

Australians travel by car, train and plane. Huge lorries pulling trailers, called road trains, move goods throughout the outback. Highway 1 circles all of Australia.

FIND OUT MORE

BOOKS

Australia (A Benjamin Blog and His Inquisitive Dog Guide),
Anita Ganeri (Raintree, 2015)

Children's Illustrated Atlas (DK Children's Atlas), Andrew Brooks
(DK Children, 2016)

Introducing Australia (Introducing Continents), Anita Ganeri
(Raintree, 2014)

WEBSITES

www.bbc.com/bitesize/articles/zf26rj6
Explore Australia's Northern Territory.

www.dkfindout.com/us/earth/continents/australasia-and-oceania
Find out more about Australasia and Oceania.

COMPREHENSION QUESTIONS

1. Describe some of the animals that live in Australia.

2. What is the name given to someone who looks after sheep or cattle on an Australian farm?

3. Can you suggest why the Melbourne Cup is called "the race that stops a nation"?

INDEX

barbecue 12

capital 4

coasts 6

deserts 6

food 12

jobs 16

kangaroos 8

koalas 8

Melbourne Cup 14

outback, the 6, 18

people 10, 12, 14, 16, 18

rainforests 6

sharks 8

size 4

snakes 8

spiders 8

sport 12, 14

transport 18

Uluru 20

wildlife 8